Invisible Journeys
Sound

Caroline Grimshaw

TEXT EDITOR IQBAL HUSSAIN
SCIENCE CONSULTANT JOHN STRINGER

TWO CAN ™

Invisible Journeys
Sound

CREATIVE AND EDITORIAL DIRECTOR
CONCEPT/FORMAT/DESIGN/TEXT
CAROLINE GRIMSHAW

TEXT EDITOR **IQBAL HUSSAIN**
SCIENCE CONSULTANT **JOHN STRINGER**

ILLUSTRATIONS
NICK DUFFY ❋ SPIKE GERRELL
CAROLINE GRIMSHAW

THANKS TO
TIM SANPHER COMPUTER IMAGERY
LAURA CARTWRIGHT PICTURE RESEARCH

TITLES IN THIS SERIES ---> ❋ SUN
❋ COMMUNICATION
❋ SOUND
❋ ENERGY

CONCEIVED AND DESIGNED BY
CAROLINE GRIMSHAW FOR
TWO-CAN PUBLISHING LTD
346 OLD STREET
LONDON EC1V 9NQ

FIRST PUBLISHED BY TWO-CAN PUBLISHING LTD IN 1998.

ISBN 1-85434-696-6 (HB) ISBN 1-85434-612-1 (PB)

DEWEY DECIMAL CLASSIFICATION 534

HARDBACK 2 4 6 8 10 9 7 5 3 1 PAPERBACK 2 4 6 8 10 9 7 5 3 1

A CATALOGUE RECORD FOR THIS BOOK IS AVAILABLE
FROM THE BRITISH LIBRARY.

PRINTED AND BOUND IN SPAIN BY GRAFICROMO S.A.

I am your Route Maestro. I will show you the way.
Look out for my two companions on your journey.

Welcome
TO
Invisible Journeys

THE Highway

Travel along the *Highway* following
a sound's journey from its source
(the sound itself) to its end (the people).

THE Byways

On your journey you will be asked
to select your own route. Choose
a *Byway* and follow the path.

THE Show Zones

The *Byways* lead you to *Show Zones*,
which contain vital information about
your trip. These may lead you further -
watch out for *Zone Overload* panels,
which are bursting with fascinating facts.
Visible Proof Spots will test your
knowledge with experiments and puzzles.
Bypass Buttons allow you to leap
forward to *Show Zones* further along
the route. They have a symbol that looks
like this. ------------>

Let's examine sound!

Bypass
BUTTON

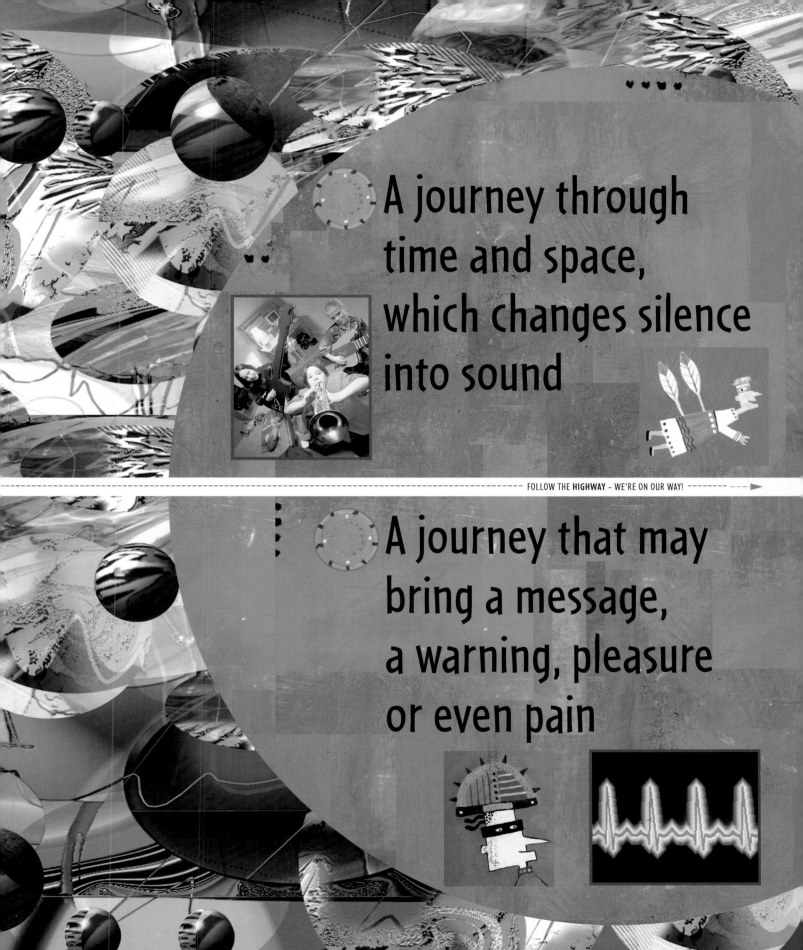

A journey through
time and space,
which changes silence
into sound

A journey that may
bring a message,
a warning, pleasure
or even pain

A whisper, the rustling of leaves, the roar of a jet engine, the boom of a bass drum – all of these are

FOLLOW THE **HIGHWAY** →

sounds

Our journey begins at the point at which sound is made.

Sounds are all around us. Let's examine what they are and where they come from.

Select
YOUR BYWAY

The Sound

1 What is sound?
(WHAT ARE SOUND WAVES?)

BYWAY TO SHOW ZONE

2 How do we describe sound?
(HOW DO WE WRITE IT DOWN?)

BYWAY TO SHOW ZONE

3 How have people studied sound?

BYWAY TO SHOW ZONE 3

4 Can we see sound?
(CAN WE FEEL IT?)

BYWAY TO SHOW ZONE 4

5 What different ways are there of making sound?

BYWAY TO SHOW ZONE 5

6 Why is sound so important to us?

BYWAY TO SHOW ZONE 6

Just think!
Not only can we hear sound, but we can also feel it – and see it too!

1

What is sound?

Sound is anything that can be heard. Every sound is made by something moving rapidly back and forth. These movements are called vibrations and are usually too small to see.

Bypass BUTTON

CAN WE FEEL SOUND VIBRATIONS? LEAP TO **SHOW ZONE 4**.

HOW DOES SOUND TRAVEL? FOLLOW THE PATH TO THE ZONE OVERLOAD.

 Visible Proof SPOT

Sound is made when an object vibrates. Place a ruler over the edge of a table and twang it. As the ruler vibrates, it produces a whirring sound. When the vibrations stop, so does the sound.

VIBRATIONS AND SOUND

※ As an object vibrates, it causes the air around it to vibrate.

VIBRATIONS BECOME SOUND
VIBRATIONS
OBJECT

※ When the vibrating air reaches our ears, the brain interprets it as sound.

Striking a drum with sticks makes it vibrate, producing a thumping sound.

Bypass BUTTON

SOUND TRAVELS THROUGH AIR, BUT IT CAN ALSO MOVE THROUGH SOLIDS AND LIQUIDS. LEAP TO **SHOW ZONE 7**.

FOLLOW THE HIGHWAY

ZONE Overload

Sound moves in waves.

What are sound waves?

If you drop a pebble into still water, waves spread out from the point where the pebble hits the surface. Sound travels through the air in a similar series of waves.

1 When a vibrating object moves outwards, it squeezes the air molecules (tiny particles) near it. This is called an area of compression.

2 As the object moves inwards, air molecules are more spread out in the space left behind. This is called an area of rarefaction.

3 Sound waves are made up of the series of compressions and rarefactions produced by the object, as it continues to move outwards and inwards.

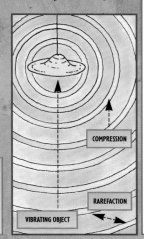
COMPRESSION
RAREFACTION
VIBRATING OBJECT

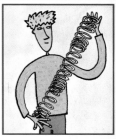 **Visible Proof** SPOT

Sound waves move by squeezing and stretching. Hold a spring toy or a coiled bangle between your hands. When you pull one end in and out, it alternately bunches together (making compressions) and stretches out (making rarefactions).

WHAT IS A DECIBEL? **BYWAY TO SHOW ZONE 2**

WHO GAVE HIS NAME TO A MEASUREMENT OF SOUND? **BYWAY TO SHOW ZONE 3**

HOW CAN WE SEE SOUND WAVES? **BYWAY TO SHOW ZONE 4**

WHAT DIFFERENT WAYS ARE THERE OF MAKING SOUNDS? **BYWAY TO SHOW ZONE 5**

WHY DO WE NEED SOUND? **BYWAY TO SHOW ZONE 6**

2

How do we describe sound?

As well as describing sound as loud or soft, we can examine its frequency and pitch, its intensity and its quality.

WHAT'S THE DIFFERENCE BETWEEN FREQUENCY AND PITCH? **BYWAY** TO **SHOW ZONE 2**

1 Frequency and pitch

❋ The **FREQUENCY** of a sound wave is the number of compressions or rarefactions a vibrating object makes in a second. Frequency is measured in hertz (Hz). One hertz equals one vibration per second.

❋ The **PITCH** of a sound is how high or low it sounds to a listener. Pitch is determined by the frequency of a sound. High-pitched sounds have higher frequencies than low-pitched sounds.

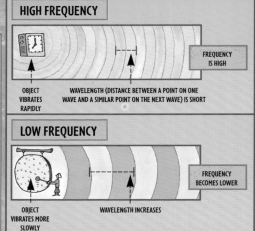

HIGH FREQUENCY

OBJECT VIBRATES RAPIDLY

WAVELENGTH (DISTANCE BETWEEN A POINT ON ONE WAVE AND A SIMILAR POINT ON THE NEXT WAVE) IS SHORT

FREQUENCY IS HIGH

LOW FREQUENCY

OBJECT VIBRATES MORE SLOWLY

WAVELENGTH INCREASES

FREQUENCY BECOMES LOWER

Bypass BUTTON

FIND OUT MORE ABOUT A MAN WHO GAVE HIS NAME TO THE UNIT USED TO MEASURE FREQUENCY. LEAP TO **SHOW ZONE 3**.

Visible Proof SPOT

Stretch various rubber bands across a hollow, metal tin. When you pluck the bands, they vibrate and produce sounds. How does the thickness and tautness of each band affect its pitch?

FOLLOW THE **HIGHWAY** AND FIND OUT ABOUT THE SPEED OF SOUND

3 The quality of the sound

❋ The way that a sound is produced determines its **SOUND QUALITY**. Musical sounds, or notes, of the same pitch and intensity sound different when played on different instruments. This is because almost every note is made up of a basic, or fundamental, note and a number of less important notes, or overtones. The overtones give the sound of each instrument its particular quality, or timbre.

Bypass BUTTON

MUSICAL INSTRUMENTS CREATE SOUNDS IN MANY WAYS. LEAP TO **SHOW ZONE 20**.

A flute produces a soft note, with a few weak overtones. The same note on a violin sounds piercing because it has many strong overtones.

FOLLOW THE PATH TO THE **ZONE OVERLOAD** TO DISCOVER HOW WE DESCRIBE SOUNDS IN WORDS AND SYMBOLS.

BYWAY TO SHOW ZONE 3

BYWAY TO SHOW ZONE 4

BYWAY TO SHOW ZONE 5

BYWAY TO SHOW ZONE 6

2 Intensity and loudness

✳ The **INTENSITY** of a sound is the amount of energy carried in the sound waves. The larger the distance a vibrating object moves from its resting position, the more intense is the sound.

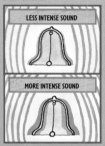

LESS INTENSE SOUND

MORE INTENSE SOUND

AMPLITUDE = DISTANCE AN OBJECT MOVES AWAY FROM ITS ORIGINAL POSITION AS IT VIBRATES

✳ The **LOUDNESS** of a sound is how strong it sounds to someone listening to it. The more intense a sound is, the louder it seems. The greater the distance between the source of the sound and the person hearing it, the quieter is the sound.

Visible Proof SPOT

Turn on a radio and ask a friend to walk away from you with the radio still playing. Notice how the sound gradually fades.

The sound of falling leaves may measure only 10 decibels.

MEASURING SOUND INTENSITY

The intensity of a sound is measured in decibels (dB). Each 10 dB added to a sound multiplies its intensity by 10. So, a 20 dB sound is 10 times as intense as a 10 dB sound, while a 30 dB sound is 100 times (10 x 10) as intense as a 10 dB sound.

EXAMINING INTENSITY

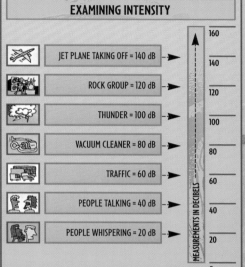

JET PLANE TAKING OFF = 140 dB	→ 160
ROCK GROUP = 120 dB	→ 140
THUNDER = 100 dB	→ 120
VACUUM CLEANER = 80 dB	→ 100
TRAFFIC = 60 dB	→ 80
PEOPLE TALKING = 40 dB	→ 60
PEOPLE WHISPERING = 20 dB	→ 40
	20
	0

MEASUREMENTS IN DECIBELS

- - - - - FOLLOW THE **HIGHWAY** - - - - ▶

Overload

Sounds can be captured on paper.

How do we write down sounds?

There are may ways of writing down or describing sounds.

IMITATING SOUNDS

We can use words that copy the sound they are describing. This is called onomatopoeia.

EXAMPLES: "CUCKOO", "BANG", "SPLASH", "HISS".

USING SIMILES

A simile is a way of describing one thing by comparing it to another.

EXAMPLE: "SHE SANG LIKE A NIGHTINGALE".

GIVING INSTRUCTIONS

Composers write down music using a special code, called notation.

✳ NOTES ARE WRITTEN ON AND BETWEEN FIVE LINES, CALLED A STAFF OR STAVE. EACH LINE AND SPACE REPRESENTS A DIFFERENT PITCH.
✳ THE SHAPE OF A NOTE SHOWS HOW LONG IT IS TO BE PLAYED.
✳ WORDS AND SIGNS DESCRIBE HOW THE MUSIC SHOULD BE PLAYED. EXAMPLES:
PIANISSIMO (PP) = VERY SOFTLY
FORTE (F) = LOUDLY
CRESCENDO (<) = GETTING LOUDER.

- - - - SOME PEOPLE SPEND THEIR LIVES STUDYING SOUND. **BYWAY** TO SHOW ZONE 3 - - - - ▶

- - - - AS WELL AS BEING HEARD, SOUND CAN BE SEEN AND FELT TOO! **BYWAY** TO SHOW ZONE 4 - - - - ▶

- - - - SOUND FROM INSIDE THE BODY! **BYWAY** TO SHOW ZONE 5 - - - - ▶

- - - - SOUND CAN WARN US OF TROUBLE AHEAD. **BYWAY** TO SHOW ZONE 6 - - - - ▶

3

How have people studied sound?

Scientists and great thinkers, or philosophers, have studied sound since ancient times. Their discoveries have changed people's understanding of how sound is produced and heard.

WHO MADE IMPORTANT DISCOVERIES ABOUT SOUND? BYWAY TO SHOW ZONE 3

1 PYTHAGORAS (580 BC – ?)

Pythagoras was a Greek philosopher and mathematician. He carried out experiments to find out how the length of a stretched string affected the sound it made when it vibrated.

2 ARISTOTLE (384–322 BC)

This Greek philosopher suggested that sound is carried to our ears by the movement of air.

3 LEONARDO DA VINCI (1452–1519)

This Italian painter and scientist helped to develop the theory that sound travels in waves.

4 GALILEO GALILEI (1564–1642)

This Italian astronomer and scientist discovered that the frequency of sound waves determines their pitch.

FOLLOW THE **HIGHWAY**

4

Can we see sound?

Machines can create pictures of sound waves, even though they are invisible in the air. We can also see the effects of sound waves.

THE OSCILLOSCOPE

An oscilloscope is a machine that shows sound waves as electrical signals. These signals appear on a screen as wavy lines, which change as the sound itself changes.

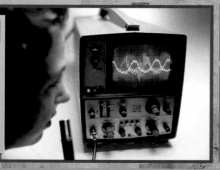

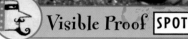

※ A stereo system often has a screen that displays the changing sound levels of a piece of music or speech.

Visible Proof SPOT

When sound waves hit an object, they may make it vibrate. Stretch a piece of plastic across a bowl and secure it with a rubber band. Sprinkle some salt on the plastic. Now make a loud sound by holding a metal pan close to the bowl and banging it. The sound waves from the lid strike the plastic and make it vibrate. This causes the salt crystals to jump.

CAN WE FEEL SOUND VIBRATIONS? FOLLOW THE PATH TO THE **ZONE OVERLOAD**.

BYWAY TO SHOW ZONE 3
BYWAY TO SHOW ZONE 4
BYWAY TO SHOW ZONE 5
BYWAY TO SHOW ZONE 6

Press a glass to a closed door, then place your ear to the bottom of the glass. You should hear sounds inside the room much louder than by just listening with your ears. Sound waves from the room are carried direct to your ear through the door and the glass.

ACOUSTICS

Acoustics is the science of sound – how it is created, transmitted and received.

5
MARIN MERSENNE (1588–1648)

This French monk and mathematician was the first to estimate the speed of sound. He asked a fellow monk to fire a gun a known distance away, then calculated how long it took for him to hear the bang after seeing the flash of the gun.

6
ROBERT BOYLE (1627–1691)

This Irish scientist showed that sound waves need some kind of matter, or medium, to travel through. He pumped out the air from a jar containing a ticking watch. When the air was completely removed, the ticking could no longer be heard.

Bypass BUTTON

THERE IS NO AIR IN SPACE, SO HOW DO ASTRONAUTS TALK TO EACH OTHER? BYPASS TO SHOW ZONE 7.

7
HEINRICH HERTZ (1857–1894)

This German scientist discovered radio waves, which paved the way for the invention of radio. The unit of frequency used for all waves and vibrations is named after him.

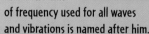
FOLLOW THE **HIGHWAY** TO FIND OUT HOW THE SPEED OF SOUND DEPENDS ON THE MEDIUM THROUGH WHICH IT TRAVELS

ZONE
Overload
Feel the ground move!

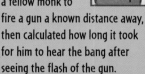

Can we feel sound?

Some sound waves are so loud and intense that they are felt as well as heard.

Heavy traffic, such as large lorries and high-speed trains, can produce powerful sound waves. Traffic generates between 60-90 dB of noise. This may penetrate the walls and windows of nearby buildings and cause the furniture inside to vibrate!

Bypass BUTTON

SOME SOUNDS CAN BE DANGEROUS. BYPASS TO SHOW ZONE 18.

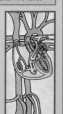

What different ways are there of making sound?

Bypass BUTTON

FIND OUT HOW PEOPLE TURN SOUND INTO SPEECH. BYPASS TO **SHOW ZONE 21.**

All sounds are caused by vibrations. These vibrations may be made in many ways – from two objects striking each other, such as a stick banging a drum, to the whistling of the wind as it blows through the trees.

THE SOUND OF A HEARTBEAT

Heart valves are flaps of skin that open and shut to control the flow of blood through the heart. The sound of a heartbeat is the sound of the valves closing when the heart squeezes out blood.

※ HEARING THE HEARTBEAT

A doctor uses a stethoscope to listen to the soft sounds of a person's heartbeat. A stethoscope is a rubber tube with a small, flat funnel at one end and a pair of earpieces at the other.

THE BUZZ OF A BEE

The buzzing sound of bees and many other flying insects is made by the vibrations of their wings beating rapidly against the air.

➤ FOLLOW THE **HIGHWAY** AND FIND OUT HOW SOUND TRAVELS

Why is sound so important to us?

Bypass BUTTON

TO DISCOVER HOW WE HEAR SOUND, BYPASS TO **SHOW ZONE 10.**

Visible Proof SPOT

Language is the most common form of communication. Without speaking, try to tell a friend about a book you have read. How easy is it to relay the information using just gestures?

People use sound to communicate with each other. Some sounds act as warning devices, while others help to catch someone's attention. Sounds can be stimulating or relaxing.

1 TIME TO COMMUNICATE

※ Early people probably communicated with one another by making basic sounds such as grunts, barks and hoots.

※ Today, almost six billion people live on the planet. There are about 6,000 different languages in the world and thousands more dialects, which are local variations of languages.

2 WATCH OUT!

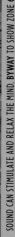

※ The ancient Celts used sound to help them in their wars against the Romans. In the heat of battle, Celtic warriors would blow large, trumpet-like instruments, called carnyxes. These produced a tremendous, screaming din that terrified the Roman soldiers!

3 LISTEN UP!

※ Some machines use devices such as bells or buzzers to attract our attention. Modern telephones have electronic bleepers that ring to let us know that someone is calling. In a cuckoo clock, a toy bird pops out of the clock and marks the time with the call of a cuckoo.

4 STIMULATING AND RELAXING

※ For hundreds of years, the steady, booming beat of drums gave courage to armies marching into battle.

※ Waves lapping against the shore, birdsong on a summer's day, the crackle of a log fire on a winter's evening – these are all sounds that many people find relaxing.

BYWAY TO SHOW ZONE 5 • BYWAY TO SHOW ZONE 5 • WHAT MAKES THE SOUND OF A HEARTBEAT? BYWAY TO SHOW ZONE 5 • SOUND CAN STIMULATE AND RELAX THE MIND. BYWAY TO SHOW ZONE 6

7

Let's look at sound waves on the move...

Select

YOUR BYWAY

HOW THE SOUND
Travels

7 Can sound travel through solid objects and liquids?
(CAN IT TRAVEL THROUGH SPACE?)

8 How fast does sound travel?
(WHAT IS A SONIC BOOM?)

9 How does sound travel from one place to another?
(WHAT IS AN ECHO?)

Imagine!
When an object making a sound travels faster than the sound itself, it produces a crashing noise called a sonic boom!

BYWAY TO SHOW ZONE 7

Bypass
BUTTON

SOUND TRAVELS AT DIFFERENT SPEEDS THROUGH DIFFERENT MATERIALS. LEAP TO SHOW ZONE 8.

FOLLOW THE PATH TO THE **ZONE OVERLOAD** TO FIND OUT ABOUT SOUND IN SPACE.

Can sound travel through solid objects and liquids?

Sound needs a medium, such as air, to travel through. It can also pass through other gases, as well as solids and liquids.

VIBRATIONS ON THE MOVE

Although most sounds reach our ears through the air, sound waves travel better through solid surfaces. American Indians used to put their ears to the ground to listen for distant hoofbeats.

FOLLOW THE **HIGHWAY** TO DISCOVER HOW WE HEAR SOUND

BYWAY TO SHOW ZONE 8

BYWAY TO SHOW ZONE 9

ZONE
Overload
Sound cannot travel through nothing at all.

Can sound travel through space?

No. In space, there is no air, nor any other medium, to carry sound waves. If you were able to shout your name in space, you would not hear a sound!

※ Radio waves do not need any medium through which to travel, which is why astronauts use radios to talk to each other.
※ To communicate in space without radios, astronauts would have to touch helmets together. Sound waves could then travel through the helmets and the air inside them.

WHAT IS THE SOUND BARRIER? **BYWAY** TO SHOW ZONE 8

HOW DOES SOUND TRAVEL? **BYWAY** TO SHOW ZONE 9

8

How fast does sound travel?

The speed of sound depends on the medium through which it travels.

LOOKING AT THE MEDIUM

The speed at which sound waves travel through a medium depends on:

1 DENSITY = how tightly matter in the medium is packed into a space

2 COMPRESSIBILITY = how easy it is to squeeze the matter into a smaller space

In general, sound travels faster through solids and liquids than through air. The molecules in solids and liquids are packed closer together and are more tightly bound than in air, so they are able to pass on sound waves more quickly.

COMPARING MEDIUMS

MEDIUM		SPEED (METRES PER SECOND)
THIS CHART SHOWS THE SPEED OF SOUND IN VARIOUS MEDIUMS		
AIR (AT 15 °C)		340
SEAWATER (AT 25 °C)		1,531
BRICK		3,650
WOOD (MAPLE)		4,110
GLASS		4,540
ALUMINIUM		5,000
STEEL		5,200

Male humpback whales sing songs that carry for hundreds of kilometres through the oceans.

The speed of sound through air is 340 metres per second. It is usually measured at sea level at 15 °C. Sound travels faster as the temperature increases. The speed of sound through air at 100 °C is 386 metres per second.

Bypass
BUTTON

THE SOUND THAT A MOVING OBJECT MAKES SEEMS TO CHANGE AS THE OBJECT PASSES BY. BYPASS TO **SHOW ZONE 10.**

------► FOLLOW THE **HIGHWAY** --------------------------------------

9

How does sound travel from one place to another?

Sound may pass along a wire as electrical signals, or through the air as radio waves.

1

Electrical signals

The American inventor Alexander Graham Bell (1847-1922) invented the telephone in 1876. It was the first machine to be able to carry voice vibrations as electrical signals.

HOW A TELEPHONE WORKS

❋ When you speak into the mouthpiece of a telephone, a microphone turns the sound waves of your voice into electrical signals.

❋ These pass down the telephone cable to the telephone of the person you are calling. There, a loudspeaker in the earpiece converts the signals back into sound waves that are very similar to your voice.

2

Radio waves

In 1895, the Italian inventor Guglielmo Marconi (1874-1937) became the first person to send radio signals as waves through the air. Before then, signals had been transmitted along electric wires.

DOES SOUND TRAVEL AT DIFFERENT SPEEDS THROUGH DIFFERENT MATERIALS? BYWAY TO SHOW ZONE 8

BYWAY TO SHOW ZONE 9

People who work underground, such as tunnel-builders, often send messages to each other by tapping on pipes. Sound travels faster and further through metal than through air.

♪ Visible Proof SPOT

...ound loses its ...nergy less rapidly ...avelling through ... solid object than ...rough air. Ask a ...riend to drop a ...in on a table. You ...robably won't ...ear it land. Now press your ear to the ...ble. This time, you should hear the ...ound transmitted through the table.

FOLLOW THE PATH TO THE ZONE OVERLOAD.

ZONE
Overload
Some aircraft break the sound barrier.

What is a sonic boom?

A sonic boom is a loud, thunder-like sound. It is made by an object travelling faster than the speed of sound.

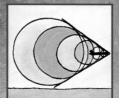

| 1 FLYING SLOWER THAN THE SPEED OF SOUND | 2 FLYING AT THE SPEED OF SOUND | 3 FLYING FASTER THAN THE SPEED OF SOUND |

1 FLYING SLOWER THAN THE SPEED OF SOUND
Sound waves spread out ahead of the plane. The waves travel faster than the plane, so people on the ground hear the plane approaching.

2 FLYING AT THE SPEED OF SOUND
The plane moves as fast as the sound waves it produces. This causes the waves to build up in front of the plane and form a shock wave.

3 FLYING FASTER THAN THE SPEED OF SOUND
The plane leaves behind a shock wave that reaches the ground and is heard as a sonic boom. The sound does not arrive until after the plane has passed.

※ A plane exceeding the speed of sound is said to have broken the sound, or sonic, barrier. Flight faster than the speed of sound is called supersonic flight. The world's only supersonic aeroplane, *Concorde*, can travel at speeds of more than 2,400 km/h.

FOLLOW THE **HIGHWAY** TO FIND OUT HOW SOUND WAVES ARE RECEIVED ----➤

There are about two billion radio sets worldwide – that's about one set for every three people.

HOW DOES A RADIO SET IN YOUR HOME PICK UP SOUNDS FROM A RADIO STATION HUNDREDS OR THOUSANDS OF MILES AWAY?

※ A microphone in the station converts the ...ounds of voices or music into electrical signals.
※ A transmitter turns the signals into radio ...aves and broadcasts them through the air ...sing a large aerial.
※ A smaller aerial on your radio set picks up ...he waves, which the radio turns back into ...lectrical signals.
※ Finally, a speaker in the radio transmits the ...lectrical signals as sounds.

FIND OUT HOW SOUND CAN BOUNCE. FOLLOW THE PATH TO THE ZONE OVERLOAD.

ZONE
Overload
Sound can be reflected or absorbed.

What is an echo?

An echo is a repetition of a sound caused by sound waves hitting a surface and being reflected.

Bypass BUTTON
REFLECTED SOUND CAN BE PUT TO IMPORTANT USES. LEAP TO **SHOW ZONE 22**.

MAKING AN ECHO

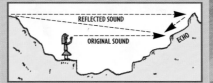

REFLECTED SOUND
ORIGINAL SOUND
ECHO

※ Smooth, hard surfaces reflect sound well. Sometimes several echoes may be heard from just one original sound. This often happens in canyons and valleys, where sound waves strike the walls at different distances and return at different times.
※ Not all surfaces reflect sound. Soft surfaces, such as fabrics and carpets, absorb sound waves so that little sound bounces back.

♪ Visible Proof SPOT

This experiment shows that hard surfaces reflect sounds well and soft surfaces do not.

1 Arrange two long cardboard tubes at the edge of a table.
2 Ask a friend to hold a large plate a few centimetres away from where the two tubes come together.
3 Place a ticking clock at the end of one tube and put your ear to the other tube.
4 Sound waves from the clock travel down the first tube, bounce off the plate and travel up the second tube to your ear.
5 Now replace the plate with a cushion. This time you cannot hear the clock as loudly – the cushion soaks up most of the sound waves.

The sound has travelled from its source to the receiver. Prepare for impact!

When sound waves reach our ears, we he all kinds of sounds and noises!

Arrival

AT DESTINATION

THE SOUND REACHES THE

People

- - - - -▶ FOLLOW THE **HIGHWAY**

- - - -▶ FOLLOW THE **HIGHWAY** - - - - - - - -▶

Select

YOUR BYWAY

Hearing
SOUND

10 How do people hear sounds?

11 Are there some sounds people cannot hear?

12 Do all living creatures hear sounds in the same way?

13 What does it mean to be deaf?

(HOW DO HEARING AIDS WORK?)

Think!

An insect's ears are never found in its head. A locust has ears on the sides of its body, while a cricket's ears are on its front legs!

10

How do people hear sounds?

Sound waves enter the ear and are changed into nerve signals. These are sent to the brain, which interprets them as sounds.

HOW DO EARS WORK? BYWAY TO SHOW ZONE 10

BYWAY TO SHOW ZONE 10

HOW THE EAR WORKS

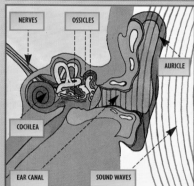

NERVES   OSSICLES

AURICLE

COCHLEA

EAR CANAL   SOUND WAVES

1 OUTER EAR The outer ear is made up of the visible part of the ear, called the auricle, and the ear canal.

WHAT HAPPENS The auricle acts as a funnel. It collects sound waves and directs them down the ear canal to the middle ear.

2 MIDDLE EAR The middle ear is made up of the eardrum and the ossicles, three tiny bones known as the hammer, the anvil and the stirrup.

WHAT HAPPENS Sound waves strike the eardrum, a flap of skin stretched tightly across the ear canal, and make it vibrate. This causes the bones in the ossicles to vibrate. The ossicles pick up and magnify the vibrations as they relay them to the inner ear.

3 INNER EAR
The inner ear is made up of the semicircular canals, which help us to balance, and a fluid-filled tube called the cochlea.

WHAT HAPPENS The vibrations create waves in the liquid in the cochlea. This movement shakes tiny hairs that line the cochlea. The hairs stimulate nerve cells, which send electrical signals, or impulses, to the brain. The brain processes the impulses into sounds.

FOLLOW THE **HIGHWAY** TO FIND OUT ABOUT SOUNDS MADE BY NATURE →

BYWAY TO SHOW ZONE 11

BYWAY TO SHOW ZONE 12

BYWAY TO SHOW ZONE 13

Bypass
BUTTON

HOW DO ANIMALS HEAR SOUNDS? FIND OUT IN **SHOW ZONE 12**.

HEARING SOUNDS DIFFERENTLY WHEN THEY ARE ON THE MOVE

The next time a police car rushes past you, listen to the pitch of its siren. As the car approaches, the pitch seems to get higher. As the car goes past, the pitch seems to get lower. To the person in the car, the pitch remains the same. This is called the Doppler effect.

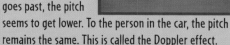

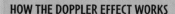

HOW THE DOPPLER EFFECT WORKS

As a police car speeds towards you, sound waves from the siren are crowded together. This increases their frequency, so you hear a higher note. When the car passes by, the waves are spaced further apart. They have a lower frequency, so you hear a lower note.

When you hold a shell to your ear, it is not the sound of the sea that you hear, but your blood as it flows through your ears. The shell blocks out most of the other sounds around you, while the air in the shell makes the sound of the blood much louder.

 Visible Proof **SPOT**

Create the Doppler effect by getting a friend on a bicycle to ride past you quickly, while blowing a whistle. Notice how the pitch of the whistle alters slightly as your friend passes you. What happens to the pitch if your friend cycles slowly?

WHAT SOUNDS ARE OUTSIDE OUR RANGE OF HEARING? **BYWAY TO SHOW ZONE 11** →

CAN ANIMALS HEAR SOUNDS THAT HUMANS CANNOT? **BYWAY TO SHOW ZONE 12** →

CAN MACHINES HELP DEAF PEOPLE TO HEAR? **BYWAY TO SHOW ZONE 13** →

11

Bypass
BUTTON
FIND OUT HOW ULTRASOUND IS USED IN MEDICINE. LEAP TO **SHOW ZONE 23.**

Are there some sounds people cannot hear?

 Visible Proof SPOT

Some sounds are too high in pitch for human ears to detect. This type of sound is called ultrasound. Other sounds are too low in pitch to be heard. This type of sound is called infrasound.

Bypass
BUTTON
MANY ANIMALS CAN HEAR SOUNDS THAT PEOPLE CANNOT HEAR. LEAP TO **SHOW ZONE 12.**

To hear notes that are just inside the human range of hearing, press the very bottom and top keys of a piano. The bottom key produces a low note with a frequency of about 30 Hz, while the top key produces a high note with a frequency of about 15,000 Hz.

ULTRASOUND	INFRASOUND
※ Sound with a frequency above the range of human hearing. ※ Frequency of more than 20,000 Hz.	※ Sound with a frequency below the range of human hearing. ※ Frequency of less than 20 Hz.

Most people can hear sounds with frequencies between 20 and 20,000 Hz. This changes as people get older. A person aged 60 years can only hear frequencies up to about 12,000 Hz.

FOLLOW THE **HIGHWAY** AND FIND OUT ABOUT ANIMALS AND THE SOUNDS THEY MAKE

12

WHAT ARE ULTRASOUND AND INFRASOUND? BYWAY TO SHOW ZONE 11

DO MOSQUITOES HAVE EARS? BYWAY TO SHOW ZONE 12

WHO HEARS WHAT?

Do all living creatures hear sounds in the same way?

Different animals hear at different frequencies. Many have ears that are quite different from human ears.

MOST ANIMALS HEAR FREQUENCIES FAR HIGHER THAN THOSE HEARD BY PEOPLE. EXAMINE THIS CHART.

CREATURE		SOUND HEARD (HERTZ)
GRASSHOPPER		100-15,000
HUMAN BEING		20-20,000
ROBIN		250-21,000
DOG		15-50,000
CAT		60-65,000
BAT		1,000-120,000
DOLPHIN		150-150,000

MOSQUITO

Mosquitoes have sound-sensitive hairs on their antennae. Sound waves cause the hairs to vibrate. This vibration passes along the mosquito's antennae.

SNAKE

Snakes have inner ears, but no outer or middle ears. The bones of a snake's skull detect vibrations and transmit them directly to the inner ears.

BYWAY TO SHOW ZONE 13 TO LEARN ABOUT DEAFNESS

13

What does it mean to be deaf?

Some people are totally deaf, which means they cannot hear any sounds. Other people are partly deaf, or hard of hearing, which means they can hear some sounds.

BYWAY TO SHOW ZONE 13

WHAT CAUSES DEAFNESS?

1 PROBLEMS WITH THE OUTER OR MIDDLE EAR
※ The ear canal can become blocked with ear wax. Doctors remove the wax by washing the ear out with jets of water.
※ If the middle ear becomes infected, it may fill with fluid. This stops the ossicles from transmitting vibrations to the inner ear.

2 PROBLEMS WITH THE INNER EAR
※ A damaged cochlea may not be able to convert sound vibrations into nerve impulses, so the brain has nothing to interpret.
※ Deafness may also occur if the auditory nerve, which carries impulses from the cochlea to the brain, is damaged.

LIVING WITH DEAFNESS

FOLLOW THE PATH TO THE ZONE OVERLOAD.

※ Speech therapists teach deaf people to lip read.
※ Many deaf people communicate using a combination of sign language and finger spelling.

※ SIGN LANGUAGE uses gestures and hand signals to represent objects and ideas.
※ FINGER SPELLING uses hand signals to represent different letters of the alphabet.

Bypass BUTTON

LOUD SOUNDS CAN DAMAGE THE EAR. BYPASS TO SHOW ZONE 18.

  Visible Proof SPOT

Try to lip read a whispered message from a friend.
Your friend should face you and speak slowly and clearly.

FOLLOW THE HIGHWAY

ZONE
Overload

Machines can improve hearing.

How do hearing aids work?

Hearing aids are devices that make sounds louder for people who are hard of hearing.

Bypass BUTTON

WHAT MACHINES DO WE USE TO AMPLIFY MUSIC? BYPASS TO SHOW ZONE 25.

※ Very loud sounds can permanently damage your hearing. Never put your ear close to a loud noise.

THE HISTORY

※ Hearing aids were first used in the 1600s. People used horn-shaped devices called ear trumpets.
※ The first electronic hearing aids, called vacuum-tube aids, appeared about 1920. They were large and difficult to carry.
※ Transistor hearing aids appeared in the 1950s and were small and cheap. They have completely replaced vacuum-tube aids.

HOW A HEARING AID WORKS

1 The earpiece of the hearing aid fits in the ear canal. The rest of the aid slips behind the ear. A small battery powers the hearing aid.

EARPIECE
BATTERY
RECEIVER
AMPLIFIER
MICROPHONE

2 The microphone converts sounds into electrical signals.

3 The amplifier increases, or amplifies, the strength of the signals.

4 The receiver turns the signals back into sounds, which should now be loud enough for the person to hear.

 Visible Proof SPOT

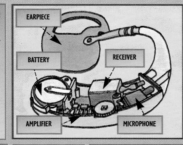

An ear trumpet amplifies sound by gathering sound waves from a large area and channelling them into the ear. Make an ear trumpet by rolling a C-shaped piece of paper into a cone. Place the narrow end of the trumpet to your ear and point the wide end at a sound.

17

14

Sound is important to the planet and all of its creatures.

Select

YOUR BYWAY

Sounds
ON PLANET EARTH

Imagine!
No one knows what dinosaurs really sounded like – we can only imagine their roars and screeches!

SOME SOUNDS ARE THE SAME WHEREVER YOU HEAR THEM. FOLLOW THE PATH TO THE **ZONE OVERLOAD**.

BYWAY TO SHOW ZONE 14

Do different part of the world have different sounds?

The sounds you hear depend on where you are and the activities that are going on around you.

FOLLOW THE **HIGHWAY** TO DISCOVER THE EFFECT THAT SOUND CAN HAVE ON PEOPLE

BYWAY TO SHOW ZONE 15

BYWAY TO SHOW ZONE 16

ZONE

Overload

That sounds familiar!

Bypass
BUTTON

ANIMALS USE SOUNDS IN MANY WAYS, FOR MANY REASONS. LEAP TO **SHOW ZONE 16**.

Are some sound recognisable everywhere?

You can identify some sounds no matter where you are in the world.

A DOG BARKING	A SIREN WAILING
Dogs make a range of sounds, including barks, yelps, growls, howls and whines. The sounds may mean different things in different situations – a whine may mean that a dog is in pain, wants something or that it wishes to play.	Most police cars, fire engines and ambulances use high-pitched sirens to alert traffic. Lighthouses and ships use low-pitched sirens, called foghorns to warn other ships about bad weather or obstacles.

1. In the rainforest

SOUNDS YOU MAY HEAR...

	The piercing screams of macaws.
	The roars of leopards.
	The hiss of snakes.
	The beating of hummingbird wings.
	The croak of tree frogs.
	The rustling of leaves.
	The patter of raindrops.

2. In the city

SOUNDS YOU MAY HEAR...

	The thud of footsteps.
	The roar of traffic.
	The honking of car horns.
	The blare of music from radios.
	Voices talking or shouting.
	The clatter of machinery.
	The banging of doors.

  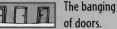

Visible Proof · SPOT

Take a walk around your neighbourhood and make a note of the different sounds you hear. Repeat the walk at various times throughout the day. Do the sounds that you hear in each case change depending on the time of day it is?

NATURE'S SOUNDS

❋ VOLCANOES
Powerful forces within the Earth create volcanoes. In 1883, Krakatau, in Indonesia, erupted with such force that the explosion was heard almost 4,800 kilometres away.

❋ WAVES
The movement of air over seas and oceans creates waves. They may lap gently as they break over each other. The

wind may whip up the water into large waves that rise and smash against each other, lashing harbour walls and grinding pebbles together on the seashore.

FOLLOW THE **HIGHWAY** ➔

LISTENING TO THE WEATHER

1 THUNDER
When air is heated by a flash of lightning, it expands rapidly and creates giant sound waves in the air. We hear these sound waves as a clap, crackle or rumble of thunder.

Visible Proof · SPOT

Blow up a paper bag and pop it by punching it. Like thunder, the bursting bag makes a loud sound as it sends sound waves hurtling through the air. The sound is created by the air molecules in the bag being rapidly squashed together and then released when the bag rips open.

2 WIND
A tornado is a powerful, twisting windstorm. Howling winds swirl in the shape of a funnel, reaching speeds of more than 320 kilometres per hour.

Bypass BUTTON

HOW CAN SOUND CAUSE AN AVALANCHE? FIND OUT IN SHOW ZONE 18.

ARE SOME SOUNDS NO LONGER HEARD? **BYWAY** TO SHOW ZONE 15 ➔

19

WHY IS SOUND SO IMPORTANT TO ANIMALS? **BYWAY** TO SHOW ZONE 16 ➔

15

Why do sounds appear and disappear through time?

Some sounds are not heard any more because whatever produced them no longer exists. Other sounds appear with the invention of machines and devices that make our lives easier.

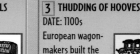
Bypass
BUTTON
TECHNOLOGY HAS CHANGE[D]
THE MACHINES WE USE TO
RECORD SOUND. BYPASS T[O]
SHOW ZONE 24.

Visible Proof SPOT

Listen to the sounds made by objects in different rooms in your home. Which sounds would you not have heard 10 years ago? You may need to ask an older brother or sister, or your parents.

THE INVENTION OF DIFFERENT FORMS OF TRANSPORT OVER THE CENTURIES CREATED MANY NEW SOUNDS.

1 SLITHERING AND SLIDING
DATE: BEFORE 5000 BC
During prehistoric times, people used sledges to drag loads along the ground. They were usually made from logs or animal skins.

2 CREAKING OF WHEELS
DATE: ABOUT 3500 BC
The people of Mesopotamia, in the Middle East, built the first wheeled vehicles. These early carts were pulled by oxen.

3 THUDDING OF HOOVES
DATE: 1100s
European wagon-makers built the first horse-drawn carriages. The iron horseshoe, invented in about 900, helped to protect horses' hooves.

→ FOLLOW THE **HIGHWAY** TO FIND OUT ABOUT THE EFFECTS OF SOUND ON PEOPLE'S LIVES

16

How do animals use sound?

Animals use sounds to tell each other who and where they are, and how they are feeling. Sound can warn of danger, signal a challenge or mark out territory. Many animals use sound to attract a mate.

1 Danger, danger!

African vervet monkeys have three main predators – eagles, leopards and snakes. To warn each other about the kind of danger they face, the monkeys use three distinct alarm calls.

PREDATOR: Eagle.
CALL: Chuckling sound.
ACTION: Dive for cover in bushes.

PREDATOR: Leopard.
CALL: Loud bark.
ACTION: Clamber up nearby trees.

PREDATOR: Snake.
CALL: High-pitched chatter.
ACTION: Stop and search the ground.

2 Look at me!

Male frogs use their voices mainly to attract mates. Each species has its own call, from croaks, grunts and clicks to squeaks, whistles and trills. The males of many species have vocal sacs in their chins or cheeks. The frogs blow air into the sacs, which inflate like balloons and amplify the sound of their voices.

BYWAY TO SHOW ZONE 15 | BYWAY TO SHOW ZONE 15 | HOW DOES A CRICKET USE ITS WINGS TO SING? BYWAY TO SHOW ZONE 16

VANISHED SOUNDS

Animals that have died out for ever are said to be extinct. The sounds once made by extinct animals – such as dinosaurs (extinct about 65 million years ago), dodos (extinct about 1680) and the zebra-like quaggas (extinct 1883) – will never be heard again.

4 CLACKETY-CLACK
DATE: 1825

The English inventor George Stephenson built the first steam locomotive. It carried passengers between the towns of Stockton and Darlington.

5 VROOM, VROOM!
DATE: 1880s

German inventors built petrol engines to power bicycles and tricycles. In the 1890s, French engineers built petrol-engined vehicles with car bodies.

Sound changes the way we experience the world.

Select
YOUR BYWAY

Impact
OF SOUND ON PEOPLE

17 What effect does sound have on people?
(WHEN DOES SOUND BECOME NOISE?)

18 Can sound be dangerous?
(HOW CAN WE REDUCE NOISE?)

19 Can sound heal?
(WHAT IS SILENCE?)

20 When does sound become music?
(WHY DO WE REMEMBER SOME GROUPS OF SOUNDS?)

BYWAY TO SHOW ZONE 17

BYWAY TO SHOW ZONE 17

FOLLOW THE **HIGHWAY**

BYWAY TO SHOW ZONE 18

BYWAY TO SHOW ZONE 19

BYWAY TO SHOW ZONE 20

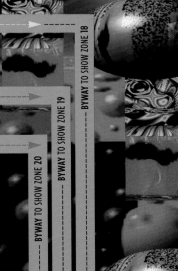

3 Watch out!

Male gelada baboons have sharp teeth, but they usually settle arguments by chattering excitedly to each other, hurling threats and noisily slapping the ground. The loser backs down by baring his teeth and gums to show fear.

4 It's me!

Male crickets "sing" to advertise their presence to females. Each type of cricket has a different song, made up of a series of trills or chirps. Crickets produce these sounds by rubbing their front wings together.

Visible Proof SPOT

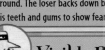

As air blows in and out of a frog's vocal sac, it causes skin stretched across the top of the sac to vibrate and produce sound. Make sound in a similar way by trapping two blades of grass between your thumbs and blowing through them.

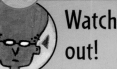

Dolphins make a range of sounds, from low frequency whistles to high frequency clicks. Dolphins even appear to use sounds to express how they are feeling, including making distress calls when they are in trouble.

Consider!

Sound can have an amazing effect on us – it can calm, excite, heal or even harm.

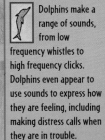

BYWAY TO SHOW ZONE 17

Bypass

BUTTON

FIND OUT MORE ABOUT MUSIC IN **SHOW ZONE 20**.

Bypass

BUTTON

CAN SOUND HEAL? LEAP TO **SHOW ZONE 19**.

SOUND CAN BECOME A NUISANCE. FOLLOW THE PATH TO THE **ZONE OVERLOAD**.

What effect does sound have on people?

Sound can create certain feelings within us. It can also affect the way we behave.

Many people respond to lively, rhythmic drum beats by automatically tapping their feet, clapping their hands or dancing. In Africa, music and dance play an important part in festivals that celebrate events such as births and harvests.

Some sounds make people wince and feel uncomfortable, such as metal scraping on metal, or fingernails on a blackboard.

A loud, sudden sound, such as a bang, may make a person yell out and even jump into the air.

Visible Proof SPOT

Films and television programmes use sounds and music to make you feel happy, excited, upset or even frightened. Watch a film or programme with your eyes closed. Can you tell what is happening just by listening to the music?

FOLLOW THE **HIGHWAY** TO DISCOVER HOW PEOPLE COPY, AMPLIFY AND USE SOUND

WHEN DOES SOUND BECOME DANGEROUS? BYWAY TO SHOW ZONE 18

Bypass

BUTTON

HOW IS MUSIC AMPLIFIED TO FILL A CONCERT HALL? FIND OUT IN **SHOW ZONE 25**.

HOW DO PEOPLE REDUCE NOISE? FOLLOW THE PATH TO THE **ZONE OVERLOAD**.

Can sound be dangerous?

A sound of 140 decibels or more crosses the threshold of pain. This means that it produces pain in the ear. Constant noise, even if it is not loud, can cause headaches, sickness and hearing loss.

An avalanche is a sudden, huge fall of snow and ice down the side of a mountain. Most avalanches happen in warmer weather, when snow melts and becomes unstable. A disturbance, such as a loud noise, can send the snow sliding.

DANGEROUS SOUND

※ A rock band can play music up to 120 dB in volume. Rock musicians and people in the audience can suffer from temporary, or even permanent, deafness.

※ Playing a personal stereo too loudly over a long period of time can damage the hearing. Sound levels inside the ears are more intense because ear phones send sound directly into the ears.

BYWAY TO SHOW ZONE 19

BYWAY TO SHOW ZONE 20

ZONE

Overload

Sound that is annoying!

When does sound become noise?

Noise is any sound that is random or unwanted.

RANDOM SOUND

※ A pleasing sound, such as a musical note, is made up of regular, gently curving sound waves.

SMOOTHLY FLOWING, PREDICTABLE WAVES

※ A random sound, or noise, such as that made by a machine, has irregular, spiky sound waves.

RANDOM, JAGGED WAVES

UNWANTED SOUND

※ Unwanted sound can be anything, from musical notes to the hammering of a drill. A sound is unwanted, or becomes noise, if a person listening to it finds it distracting, annoying, unpleasant or loud.

ELECTRICAL NOISE

※ Electrical noise is unwanted sound that is produced by radiation and disturbances in the air. These are caused by many things, including lightning, the Sun, telephones and computers. Electrical noise interferes with the reception of transmitted signals.

LUNAR LISTENING

Astronomers use radio telescopes on Earth to tune in to signals from space. The telescopes have to separate the signals from electrical noise in the atmosphere. In the future, astronomers may build observatories on the far side of the Moon, which is shielded from the Earth's noise.

Visible Proof SPOT

Tune in to different radio stations. The hissing sound you hear on some stations is electrical noise interfering with the radio signals.

------- FOLLOW THE **HIGHWAY** ----->

ZONE

Overload

Protect yourself from pain!

How can we reduce noise?

Noise pollution is the making of noise that is unpleasant to people near it. It may come from machinery, cars, planes or even other people. Noise pollution can be controlled in a number of ways.

Bypass BUTTON

FIND OUT MORE ABOUT SILENCE. BYWAY TO SHOW ZONE 19.

1 MAKING LAWS

Many countries have laws that forbid people to make noises above certain decibels during the evening. Some laws set the upper sound levels for vehicles such as lorries. Other laws set sound levels in factories, to protect the health of the workers.

2 PROTECT YOURSELF

People who are surrounded by loud noises protect their ears by wearing ear protectors, such as ear plugs or ear muffs. Ear muffs have a thick layer of padding to absorb sound.

3 PEACE AND QUIET

Buildings can be insulated from outside noise by having thick walls, well-sealed doors and double-glazed windows.

A DOUBLE-GLAZED WINDOW IS MADE OF TWO PANES OF GLASS.

SOUND DOES NOT TRAVEL AS EASILY THROUGH THE AIR BETWEEN THE PANES AS IT DOES THROUGH GLASS.

FIGHTING NOISE WITH ANTI-NOISE

※ Two noises can be added together to create silence! A microphone measures the sound wave of a noise, then a computer creates a mirror image of the wave and plays it back. The two sounds overlap and cancel each other out. This method is called anti-noise.

THE PEAKS (HIGHS) IN THE ORIGINAL SOUND WAVE CORRESPOND TO TROUGHS (LOWS) IN THE GENERATED WAVE.

IS THERE REALLY SUCH A THING AS SILENCE? **BYWAY** TO SHOW ZONE **19** ----->

------ WHEN DOES A GROUP OF SOUNDS BECOME MUSIC? **BYWAY** TO SHOW ZONE **20** ----->

19

Can sound heal?

Sound can relax us and make us calm. Some people believe that sounds have properties that make us feel better and more healthy.

A CALMING EFFECT

Mothers often soothe crying babies by talking or singing to them in hushed tones. Babies respond particularly well to low notes and repeated sounds.

MUSIC THERAPY

Some hospitals use music to stimulate patients. Patients may let out pent-up emotions by shouting, laughing, crying or dancing in response to music. Others sing or play musical instruments to help develop better control of their breathing and muscles.

ANCIENT SOUNDS

The Chinese use sound as part of Chi Kung, the ancient art of self-healing. Chi Kung teaches that sounds can strengthen and heal vital organs in the body. Each organ has its own healing sound and position. Chi Kung is also used to relax the mind and body.

Visible Proof SPOT

Make the sounds of Chi Kung to relax yourself. Stand in the positions shown and repeat each sound three times, using long, drawn-out breaths.

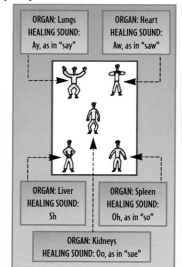

ORGAN: Lungs
HEALING SOUND: Ay, as in "say"

ORGAN: Heart
HEALING SOUND: Aw, as in "saw"

ORGAN: Liver
HEALING SOUND: Sh

ORGAN: Spleen
HEALING SOUND: Oh, as in "so"

ORGAN: Kidneys
HEALING SOUND: Oo, as in "sue"

DO SOME PEOPLE LIVE IN SILENCE? FOLLOW THE PATH TO THE **ZONE OVERLOAD**.

FOLLOW THE **HIGHWAY** TO DISCOVER HOW PEOPLE ORGANISE SOUND INTO SPEECH

20

When does sound become music?

Music is sound arranged into interesting or pleasing patterns. Musical sounds, or notes, may be produced by human voices, musical instruments, machines and even nature.

Bypass BUTTON

WHAT TYPE OF INSTRUMENT IS A SYNTHESISER? LEAP TO **SHOW ZONE 26**.

COMPOSING

A composer selects certain sounds and combines them to create a piece of music. How the music sounds depends on:
❋ the composer's skill and talent.
❋ the musical instruments available.
❋ the musical traditions of the country.
❋ the function of the piece of music.

MAKING MUSIC

When an instrument is played, part of it is set vibrating. Every instrument produces a different pattern of vibrations and sound waves. These patterns can be recorded as wave patterns on an oscilloscope.

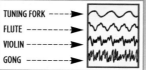

TUNING FORK
FLUTE
VIOLIN
GONG

1 WIND INSTRUMENTS

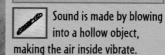 Sound is made by blowing into a hollow object, making the air inside vibrate.

A flute player blows air across a hole. To make notes of different pitches, the player presses keys that cover holes in the instrument. This changes the length of the column of vibrating air inside the flute.

2 STRING INSTRUMENTS

 Strings are plucked, bowed, strummed or struck, causing them to vibrate.

A violin player produces notes by drawing a bow, made from horsehair, across the strings. The bow makes the strings vibrate and give out sounds, which are then amplified by the hollow body of the violin.

BYWAY TO SHOW ZONE 19

HOW DO MUSICAL INSTRUMENTS MAKE SOUNDS? BYWAY TO SHOW ZONE 20

Overload

When sound disappears.

What is silence?

Silence is the absence of any sound.

TOTAL SILENCE

✻ True silence only exists when there are no molecules to transmit sound waves from one place to another.
✻ If all the air is removed from a container, it becomes a vacuum. Sound waves cannot travel through a vacuum.
✻ Human beings cannot experience silence because we cannot exist in a vacuum.

There is never total silence on Earth. There is always some sound to be heard. Deserts are among the quietest places on Earth. But even they have sounds of insects that live there and grains of sand sliding over each other.

Bypass
BUTTON

CAN YOU COMPOSE MUSIC FROM SILENCE? LEAP TO SHOW ZONE 27.

LIVING IN SILENCE

Monks and nuns are people who devote their whole lives to religion. Many monks and nuns observe a rule of silence, which means that they spend a large part of their time in silent prayer.

PYRAMID POWER

✻ The King's Chamber in the Great Pyramid at Giza, Egypt, is extremely well sound-proofed. If you stood perfectly still inside the chamber, you would hear just the sound of your own breathing. Soon you would also hear a loud rushing noise, like a waterfall. It would be the sound of the blood flowing through your body, echoed many times by the walls of the chamber!

FOLLOW THE **HIGHWAY** ---►

Visible Proof SPOT

Make your own wind instrument. Fill several glass bottles with different amounts of water. Blow gently across the tops of the bottles. The air inside each bottle vibrates and makes a different musical note. The more air there is in a bottle, the slower it vibrates and the lower the note.

FOLLOW THE PATH TO THE ZONE OVERLOAD.

3

KEYBOARD INSTRUMENTS

Keyboard instruments have a series of keys connected mechanically to a device that produces sound.

Pressing the keys of a piano keyboard activates levers that move small, padded, wooden hammers. These strike metal strings in the piano, which vibrate to produce notes.

4

PERCUSSION INSTRUMENTS

Percussion instruments include anything that can be shaken, hit, clicked or scraped.

Striking timpani, or kettledrums, with mallets produces a deep, echoing sound. A player can change the pitch by pressing a pedal, which tightens or relaxes the skin of the drum.

Overload

Keeping musical memories.

REMEMBERING TUNES

✻ We remember some songs and tunes because they mean something to us. They can recreate memories and emotions.
✻ Songs often have catchy choruses. These are known as "hooks", because they are easy to hum and remember.

Bypass
BUTTON

HOW DO WE CONTROL LIVE SOUND? BYPASS TO SHOW ZONE 25.

Why do we remember some groups of sounds?

A random collection of sounds is difficult to remember because it is unpredictable. Music is easier to remember because it is usually made up of patterns of sounds.

People use sound to communicate and to explore the world.

Select
YOUR BYWAY

Using
SOUND

SHOW ZONE

21

BYWAY TO SHOW ZONE 21

What is the most important way that people use sound?

Humans organise sounds into words, which allow us to communicate with one another.

We can use speech to show affection.

Bypass BUTTON
HOW DO SINGERS MAKE THEIR VOICES LOUDER? LEAP TO **SHOW ZONE 25**.

FOLLOW THE **HIGHWAY** TO FIND OUT HOW WE RECORD AND PLAY BACK SOUND

BYWAY TO SHOW ZONE 22

SHOW ZONE

22

BYWAY TO SHOW ZONE 23
BYWAY TO SHOW ZONE 24
BYWAY TO SHOW ZONE 25
BYWAY TO SHOW ZONE 26
BYWAY TO SHOW ZONE 27

How is sound used to explore the oceans?

HOW DO WE USE SOUND TO SHOW US WHAT IS HAPPENING INSIDE OUR BODIES? BYWAY TO SHOW ZONE 23

LANGUAGE

Humans are the only animals to use sound to create a spoken language, or speech. The word 'language' comes from the Latin word '*lingua*', meaning tongue. All languages have certain things in common.

SOUND-PATTERN = the sounds that the human speech organs can make. Most languages have between 20 and 60 of these sounds.

WORDS = sound-patterns that have a specific meaning. Words may represent objects, actions or ideas.

GRAMMAR = the rules by which words change their forms and are combined into sentences. Each language has its own grammar.

TO FIND OUT HOW WE USE OUR MOUTHS TO SPEAK, FOLLOW THE PATH TO THE **ZONE OVERLOAD**.

We can use speech to show aggression.

ZONE

Overload

It's good to talk to each other!

1 When you breathe in, muscles in the larynx (L) relax the vocal cords – small folds of tissue that stretch across the larynx (X).

2 When you speak, the muscles tighten the vocal cords (X). As air passes over the cords, it makes them vibrate and produce sound.

How do people speak?

The sound of the voice is produced mainly by the vibration of the vocal cords. The mouth, tongue, teeth and lips shape the sound into words.

Visible Proof SPOT

Stretch the neck of a blown-up balloon between your fingers. As the air escapes, it makes the neck vibrate and produce a shrieking sound. Change its pitch by tightening or relaxing your grip. The neck of the balloon acts like the vocal cords and your fingers act like the larynx muscles.

SHOW ZONE

23

Dolphins use a technique called echolocation to locate fish and underwater obstacles. Scientists use a similar principle to explore the oceans.

WHAT IS ECHOLOCATION?

✳ A dolphin produces short bursts of ultrasound, which bounce off objects and create echoes. The dolphin listens to the echoes to work out the size, distance and direction of the object.

✳ A ship's sonar device sends waves of ultrasound into the water. The time taken for the sound waves to be reflected back from the ocean bed, or from obstacles in their path, indicates the depth of the ocean bed or the obstacles.

BYWAY TO SHOW ZONE 23

How is sound used in medicine?

Doctors use ultrasound to examine the inside of a patient's body.

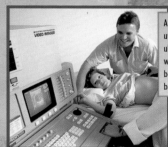

A scanner is able to show an image of an unborn baby inside its mother. It transmits ultrasound waves into the mother's womb, where they are reflected by the baby's body. The scanner interprets the echoes to build up a picture of the baby on a screen.

Ultrasound can also help to detect cancer, heart disease and other conditions.

HOW DO WE STORE SOUND? **BYWAY TO SHOW ZONE 24**

HOW DOES AN AMPLIFIER WORK? **BYWAY TO SHOW ZONE 25**

HOW DO WE USE MACHINES TO REPLICATE SOUNDS? **BYWAY TO SHOW ZONE 26**

SOUND CAN CREATE WORKS OF ART AND MOVE PEOPLE. **BYWAY TO SHOW ZONE 27**

24

What machines do we use to record sound?

Bypass BUTTON

FIND OUT HOW SOUNDS CAN BE MADE ELECTRONICALLY. LEAP TO **SHOW ZONE 26**.

For centuries, people could only listen to music live – as it was being played. From the 1870s, it became possible to record music. Today, sound can be stored in many ways and then played back at any time.

1 MECHANICAL RECORDING

In 1877, the American inventor Thomas Edison (1847-1931), pictured above, invented the first practical sound-recording machine, the phonograph. Sound made into a mouthpiece caused a needle to vibrate. This etched a groove in a foil-covered rotating cylinder. The phonograph developed into the record player, which stores sounds as jagged waves in a spiral groove on a plastic disc.

2 MAGNETIC RECORDING

In magnetic recording, sound is stored on audio tape, a thin plastic ribbon coated with metallic particles that can be magnetised. A tape recorder receives sound as electrical signals. These signals change the strength of the magnetic field around the recording head. As the tape travels past the head, the field magnetises the particles on the tape into a pattern like that of the sound waves.

3 DIGITAL RECORDING

Digital recording machines turn sound into a numerical, or digital, code. Each number in the code gives the height of a sound wave at a given point. Digital code may be stored on compact disc (CD), digital audio tape (DAT) or digital compact cassette (DCC).

Digital code is recorded on the surface of a CD as millions of tiny pits which are laid out in a spiral track.

FOLLOW THE PATH THE **ZONE OVERLO**

FOLLOW THE **HIGHWAY** TO FIND OUT HOW MACHINES COPY OR SAMPLE SOUNDS

25

How do we make sounds louder?

Singers and musicians use machines called amplifiers to make their voices and music louder. Record, cassette and disc players contain small amplifiers that strengthen electrical signals.

WHAT DID THOMAS EDISON INVENT? BYWAY TO SHOW ZONE 24

WHAT IS AN AMPLIFIER? BYWAY TO SHOW ZONE 25

❄ A microphone converts the sound waves of the singer's voice into weak electrical signals.

❄ An amplifier uses electronic components called transistors to make stronger copies of the signals.

❄ The transistors feed the strengthened signals to the speaker.

❄ The speaker turns the signals back into sound waves, which are now much louder.

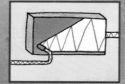
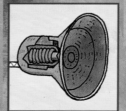

BOOSTING SIGNALS

A tape recorder uses an amplifier to boost the weak electrical signals from the microphone before they can be recorded. During playback, weak signals are again strengthened by an amplifier to make them strong enough to drive the speakers.

SOME SOUNDS CAN BE RECREATED IN SIMPLE WAYS. **BYWAY** TO SHOW ZONE 26

HOW DO CINEMAS USE SOUND? **BYWAY** TO SHOW ZONE 27

How do we replay stored sound?

Sound stored on record, tape or disc is played back through speakers, devices that turn electrical signals back into sound.

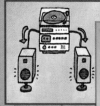

STEREOPHONIC SOUND

Music is usually recorded by using at least two microphones, spaced apart. The recordings are then combined and played back through at least two speakers, also spaced apart. This produces stereophonic sound, a lifelike sound that has depth and direction.

LISTENING TO A RECORD

As a record spins on the record player, a needle, called a stylus, rides along the groove. The stylus follows the waves in the groove and vibrates. These vibrations are turned into electrical signals, which speakers convert back into sound.

LISTENING TO A TAPE

When a tape is played back in a tape recorder, it passes the playback head. The magnetic patterns on the tape produce electrical signals in the head. The signals are relayed to speakers, where they are broadcast as sound.

LISTENING TO A DISC

A laser beam scans the surface of a CD as it spins at high speed. The pits on the disc scatter the beam, while the flat areas reflect it. A detector turns these flashes of light into electrical signals, which speakers turn back into sound.

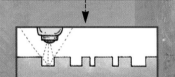

Two ears give us stereophonic hearing, which means we can tell where a sound is coming from. Shut your eyes and ask a friend to clap in different places around you. You should be able to locate the sound just by listening. How easy is it if you cover up one ear?

FOLLOW THE PATH TO THE ZONE OVERLOAD.

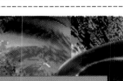

[A mega]phone is a [d]evice that [a]mplifies the [vo]ice. It focuses [so]und waves [fo]rward and stops [th]em spreading [o]ut too much. [M]ake a megaphone by rolling a [fan]-shaped piece of paper into a cone [a]nd securing it with tape. Speak into [th]e narrow end of the cone.

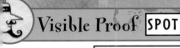

How do we control live sound?

The acoustics of a room are affected by:
* its size and shape
* the materials on its walls and ceilings
* its ability to keep out unwanted sound
* its ability to control reflected sound

Amplifiers can only control the volume of sound. The quality of sound that is heard depends a lot on the room or building in which it is played. This is known as architectural acoustics.

REFLECTION AND ABSORPTION

A concert hall or theatre is designed to provide good architectural acoustics. Panels, discs or balls hanging from the ceiling reflect the sound waves towards the audience. Some sound waves are absorbed by the chairs, curtains, carpets and even people's clothes.

26

How do we imitate sound?

Some machines and devices can copy sounds and then use them in new and exciting ways.

SYNTHESISERS

A synthesiser is an electronic instrument, usually played by means of a keyboard. A synthesiser can reproduce the sounds of traditional instruments, such as the flute or guitar. It can also create completely new sounds. Electronic components inside the synthesiser generate electrical signals that produce the sounds.

Many pop and rock artists and groups use synthesisers in their music.

SAMPLING

A sampler is a device that can digitally record any sound, from birdsong to breaking glass. The sound is then played back using a keyboard. A synthesiser can change the digital code of a sampled sound to produce sounds of different pitch and quality.

SOUND EFFECTS

Sound-effects specialists are people who create sounds for radio and television programmes. The use computers, synthesisers and samplers to crea most of their sound effects. They may also use everyday objects to make convincing sound effec such as thunder or galloping horses.

→ FOLLOW THE **HIGHWAY** TO THE END OF YOUR JOURNEY

27

How do artists use sound?

Musicians, performers and visual artists use sound to convey messages, feelings and experiences.

BYWAY TO SHOW ZONE 26

BYWAY TO SHOW ZONE 27

CONDUCTING SILENCE

In 1952, the American composer John Cage (1912-1992) wrote a work called *4' 33"*. It requires the performer to sit silently at a piano for 4 minutes and 33 seconds, without playing a note. The audience is invited to listen to sounds in the hall, such as the lid being raised or people coughing, and also to noises from outside.

SOUND AS ART

In her work *Mutual Interest* (1997), the Israeli artist Michal Rovner shows footage of birds in flight accompanied by the sound of beating wings. The film is projected in a small room, with the sound played at full volume. It echoes off the walls and, to a listener, sounds like whirring helicopter blades or gunfire.

SOUND AND MOVING IMAGES

❋ SILENT FILMS
The first films were shown publicly in the mid-1890s. Early film-makers could not match sound to the pictures, so cinemas employed pianists or orchestras to accompany the images on screen.

❋ THE "TALKIES"
The first successful film to use recorded sound was *The Jazz Singer* (1927), starring Al Jolson. Sound that had been mechanically recorded on a disc was played along in time with the film strip.

❋ SOUND-ON-FILM
By 1929, most films used a system called sound-on-fil Electronic signals recorded the sound directly on to th film strip.

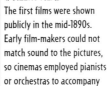

You can make realistic sound effects using simple materials.

THUNDER = flap a large sheet of thick card.

RAINFALL = pour dried peas on to a slanted metal tray.

GALLOPING HORSES = clap two halves of a coconut shell together; for a jingling harness, shake a bunch of keys.

WALKING ON SNOW = squeeze and twist a roll of cotton wool.

MARCHING ARMY = rhythmically shake a box of small stones.

BURNING OBJECT = crumple sweet wrappers and snap dried twigs.

DIGITAL SOUND

Modern cinemas use a complicated arrangement of many speakers to produce extremely realistic, three-dimensional sound, called surround-sound. The sound itself is recorded digitally along the edge of the film strip.

A TYPICAL SURROUND-SOUND SYSTEM

LEFT SURROUND   RIGHT SURROUND

CENTRE SURROUND

From the point at which

sound

is made to the Impact Zone – you!

The rumble of traffic, the buzz of a bee, the blast of a trumpet... a journey that can elevate, educate, irritate, entertain and move us.

Think!

As sound technology advances, and as further uses for ultrasound and infrasound are developed, sound will have an increasing effect on our planet. It will create a richer environment for us to live in.

Invisible Journeys
Sound
Index